D0717353

THE LIFE & TIMES OF
JOSEPH STALIN

THE LIFE & TIMES OF

Joseph Stalin

BY
Ian Schott

This edition printed for, Shooting Star Press Inc, 230 Fifth Avenue, Suite 1212, New York, NY 10001

Shooting Star Press books are available at special discount for bulk purchases for sales promotions, premiums, fund-raising or educational use. Special editions or book excerpts can also be created to specification. For details contact – Special Sales Director, Shooting Star Press Inc., 230 Fifth Avenue, Suite 1212, New York, NY 10001

This edition first published by Parragon Books
Produced by Magpie Books Ltd, 7 Kensington Church Court, London W8 4SP
Copyright © Parragon Book Service Ltd 1994
Cover picture & illustrations courtesy of: Mary Evans Picture Library; Associated Press.

ISBN 1 57335 053 2
A copy of the British Library Cataloguing in Publication Data is available from the British Library.

Typeset by Hewer Text Composition Services, Edinburgh
Printed in Singapore by Printlink International Co.

RISE OF A BUREAUCRAT

Joseph Vissarionovich Djugashvili was born on 21 December 1879 at Gori, Georgia. The name 'Stalin', meaning 'man of steel', was a pseudonym he adopted later in life, only one of the dozen aliases and code-names he used during the years he spent as a political agitator.

His family were of peasant stock. Both his parents were illiterate, and had only been liberated from serfdom in 1864, after which his father had become a penurious cobbler. Stalin was the only one of their four children to survive infancy. At the age of five he contracted smallpox which left him pock-marked for life, though his scars were air-brushed out of all official photographs. The family lived in one room, in miserable circumstances exacerbated by his father's drunkenness and violence.

Stalin's mother was determined that he should become a priest, and sent him to a Church school. When Tsarist education policy decreed that Georgian was not to be taught, Stalin was one of the principal leaders of a series of school rebellions. He also developed a fixation for the heroic figure of Koba, a Georgian outlaw who had defied the region's Russian rulers and whose story was the stuff of popular romance. For the next twenty years he insisted on being called Koba, only establishing his identity as the 'man of steel' when the Communists were firmly entrenched.

Stalin subsequently attended a seminary at Tiflis, where a training for the priesthood brought out a peculiar rigidity in his thought. His subsequent writings and speeches have a distinctly theological flavour to them, seeing matters in terms of black and white, or good and evil. The seminary was a repressive institution, in which the pupils plotted and the monks spied. Stalin learned to lie proficiently, and his adolescent psyche was shaped by this environment in which suspicion, confession, fear and treachery dominated. He became cynical both about religion and human nature. He was introverted and solitary and took comfort from reading the works of Karl Marx, from whose philosophy he was to shape his own doctrines, as harsh as the religion he rejected.

In his fifth year he was expelled as a trouble-maker. He was unconcerned. While at the seminary, he had joined a group of political activists, and he now began to disseminate Marxism among railway workers.

Over the next seventeen years, Stalin lived on the fringes of society as a political undesirable. He was arrested seven times and exiled to remote Russian territories on six of these occasions. Four times he escaped. In between arrests, he married his first wife, Ekaterina Svanidze, in 1906; they had a son, Yakov, who was later to die in a Nazi concentration camp, disowned by his father for surrendering.

Stalin and Ekaterina's married life was happy, but impoverished and brief. Stalin scribbled Marxist tracts; Ekaterina, who took no interest in politics, hoped that he would give it up and get a proper job. But, barely a year after their wedding, she died of typhus. Stalin wept at her funeral, to general surprise – he already had a reputation for self-control and coldness. In 1938 he would have his brother-in-law shot, along with those others who had known him in his youth.

In the early part of the century, the embryonic Russian revolutionary movement was a hybrid of conflicting factions united under the banner of Marxism. The most significant figure was Vladimir Ilich Ulyanov, known from 1901 as Lenin, the leader of the Bolshevik faction. Lenin was not prepared to wait for history to produce the socialist utopia, as Marx had prophesied it must; he was prepared to use force to accelerate the process. In this, he was opposed by moderate factions, the Mensheviks in particular. Stalin was Lenin's man, and quite different from the other Bolsheviks, many of whom were widely-travelled, sophisticated intellectuals from middle-class backgrounds. They chose socialism for philosophical reasons; Stalin was driven by hatred fuelled by personal experience of repression, cruelty and deprivation.

Stalin's base for his early revolutionary activities was his home region around the Caucasus. In addition to agitating, he organized hold-ups and bank robberies to fund Lenin.

Such pragmatism impressed Lenin. In 1912,

he had Stalin elected to the Bolshevik Central Committee.

Later, under Stalin's rule, Soviet historians would portray him as Lenin's right-hand man during the 1917 Revolution, but Stalin spent most of the time from 1912 to 1917 exiled in Siberia. His most significant single action of the period was to assist in the launch of the official Bolshevik newspaper, *Pravda*.

In 1922 Stalin was elected General Secretary of the Communist Party. This was to remain his highest official position until the circumstances of war obliged him to assume the position of Prime Minister in 1941.

His caution in accepting prominent positions was characteristic; he was careful to avoid any possibility of being held responsible for failure. Certainly it was he who gave the orders, but he controlled the State from a position of security to the rear of an advance guard of expendable figure-heads, who were liable to be shot as scapegoats if necessary.

The position of General Secretary of a one-party system was the key to power. The holder could make Party appointments, and only Party members could obtain high rank within the vast government bureaucracy. Rank brought privileges in housing, subsistence and entertainment; Stalin held the key to all these.

As General Secretary, Stalin also had the right to identify and eliminate heretics who deviated from the gospel of Lenin. How that gospel was interpreted was his decision.

Amid the terrible years of the Russian Civil War, and the first, improvised steps of the Communist State, Lenin continued to value Stalin's 'ability to exert pressure'.

Conditions were awful; in 1923, when Russia's population was totted up, it was found to be some 30 million short of expectations. The First World War, civil war, famine, disease and economic collapse had set the country back a century or more. Lenin needed organizers, and leaned on Stalin. Certainly he was not blind to Stalin's faults; but he underestimated, as did the other Bolsheviks, the scale of the bureaucratic empire they were permitting Stalin to build.

Others took on high-profile challenges; Stalin stayed quiet and close to his power base. He was the only man who understood how the various organs of state really functioned. He linked these anonymous bureaus, and staffed them with his acolytes, so that the whole structure of government might be swayed by his vote.

He held positions on the Supreme War Council and the Central Committee of the Communist Party. He was also Commissar for Nationalities, which made him the Central Committee's representative in all dealings with the the regions outside central Russia.

In addition, he was a member of the Politburo and the Orgburo – the policy-making and organizational committees – and was Commissar of the Workers' and Peasants' Inspectorate.

By the time Lenin realized his mistake he was too ill to do anything. 'Comrade Stalin,' he wrote in vain, 'having become General Secretary, has concentrated limitless power in his hands, and I am not sure that he will always manage to use this power with sufficient caution.'

During Lenin's last sickness, Stalin placed him under virtual house arrest. Lenin wrote a last letter to Stalin, condemning him for his rudeness and breaking off relations. Stalin wrote back, denying any guilt. The two never met again. Stalin kept Lenin's letter in his desk drawer until he died. It was to be joined by many angry and bewildered letters from others he would turn on.

Trotsky, whom Lenin favoured too late, failed to take advantage of the swing in

Stalin as a young man

Revolutionaries storm a building in St Petersburg

opinion. When Lenin died in January 1924, Stalin was still in power. Stalin cried at Lenin's funeral, but was privately jubilant. He thereafter adopted the mantle of Lenin, and every word that Lenin had spoken was regurgitated to defend Stalin's own policies. Current affairs did not distract him from his personal need to control. He confided in nobody, remained principally silent, and would always speak last at meetings in order to criticize the speeches of others without having to put his own ideas on the block. His oblique speech was cryptic and menacing.

Stalin was only interested in the exercise of power, not the trappings. He lived an austere life. Though he had married again, to Nadezhda Alliluyeva, a committed Communist twenty-two years younger than him, he took only a passing interest in his wife, with whom he had two children, Vasily and Svetlana.

In Stalin's early years of power, Nadezhda looked after his modest country home, which overflowed with weekend parties of officials, and had some degree of happiness. Over the subsequent years relations became strained, and Nadezhda several times threatened to leave Stalin. In 1932, when she realized the extent of the suffering his regime was inflicting on the people, Nadezhda shot herself. Gazing into her open coffin, Stalin did not cry. He stood in silence. 'She left me as an enemy,' he commented, walking away.

In the 1920s, Stalin pursued the twin policies of industrialization and the enforced 'collectivization' of land. The latter was an ideological assault on the traditional folk-culture and class composition of the agricultural communities of Russia and its allied territories. These communities constituted 80 per cent of the population, presenting the greatest potential threat to Stalin's authority.

The smallholdings of peasants were amalgamated into large, State-controlled farms. Whole classes of rural society were liquidated, evicted and starved to death. On Stalin's own admission the policy cost 10 million lives, though the true figure is probably much higher. Kulaks, the wealthier peasants responsible for producing the majority of the Soviet Union's food supplies, were exterminated – shot out of hand or dumped in the middle of the Siberian wastes, where they were certain to perish.

In the Ukraine, which Stalin was determined to make subject to his will, 5 million starved to death. There was food, but the State took it from them, demanding ever-higher quotas. When catastrophe came, Stalin refused to release grain, and stockpiles of it rotted in railway yards while heaps of corpses rotted at the roadside. No word of the famine was allowed in the press and no mention of it was made in public or private. All offers of overseas aid were refused. The Ukraine was cordoned off and no one was allowed to leave.

Throughout the Soviet Union a mere 240,000 State farms replaced over 25 million private holdings; they were hopelessly inefficient, and the Soviet Union suffered from food shortages until its dissolution in the 1990s.

Stalin sought only the control that centralization brought. Inefficiency was denied, with the aid of bogus statistics. The same lies accompanied the industrialization, which proceeded by means of an interminable string of Five-Year Plans, backed up with the shooting of those managers who failed to deliver, or to massage the statistics to show that they had done so.

'One aspect of the history of the old Russia', pronounced Stalin, 'was the repeated beatings she suffered for falling behind, for her backwardness . . . We are fifty to a hundred years behind the advanced countries . . . we must make good this distance in ten years. Either do this or they will crush us . . .'

The historical basis for this argument was incontrovertible. But Stalin's policies were motivated by his personal insecurities, and implemented through fear. He was determined to demonstrate that the Soviet Union could survive in isolation, which contradicted the international visions of Marx and Lenin.

THE TERROR

All dissent was eliminated. At first Stalin's opponents were not shot, only disgraced and expelled from the Communist Party.

They were all the old, intellectual Bolsheviks whom he had so envied: Trotsky, Bukharin, Rykov, Kamenev and Zinoviev. 'Our general mood was one of healthy optimism,' recalled Alexander Barmine of the years before the Terror. 'We were sure of ourselves and the future. We believed that in a few years our socialist country would be able to offer the world an example of a society founded on principles of liberty and equality.'

All this changed with the assassination of Sergei Kirov.

Stalin had known Kirov, an old Bolshevik since the Revolution of 1917. Kirov was a popular figure, whose good nature and warmth Stalin had found attractive and had been at pains to associate himself with. He called Kirov his friend and beloved brother, and their families had holidayed together.

In January 1934, the Communist Party held its seventeenth Congress, the Congress of Victors. Stalin read the conference a lengthy report on the success of the Five-Year Plan,

Lenin speaks to a crowd of Bolsheviks

A revolutionary poster

and, giving a brief version of the Party's past internal stuggles, declared it to be united as never before.

This was a challenge to his critics, for there was some apprehension within the Party about the extent of Stalin's influence, particularly among the Bolsheviks of Lenin's school. Though these now formed only a fraction of the Party's total membership, they constituted the majority of delegates to the conference, and the core of the Party leadership. Though the general tone of the conference was ostensibly adulatory, in private, regional representatives discussed the disastrous effects of Stalin's policies. But his power was such that he could not be entirely dispensed with; in any case, to do so would be to acknowledge to the world the failure of Communist policies.

It was delicately suggested that Stalin should be elevated to a symbolic role – Chairman of the Central Committee, for example, where he might concern himself more with foreign, military and State business, leaving domestic policy to his successor, who might be Kirov.

Stalin was alert to the changing mood, and any such manoeuvre was for the time ruled out. Then, on 1 December 1934, Kirov was shot dead in the Party Headquarters at the Smolny Institute, Leningrad.

There were a number of peculiarities about the assassination which pointed to the involvement of the authorities. The killer, Nikolayev, was an unstable man, who claimed to be acting on nothing more than a long-standing personal grudge. He felt that he had been unfairly excluded from authority within the Party. His grievances were well known; he had twice been arrested while carrying a gun in Kirov's vicinity, but had been released on both occasions at the insistence of the NKVD, the secret police.

On this occasion he found that the guards who were customarily stationed on each floor of the Smolny Institute had been withdrawn, and that Kirov was without his personal bodyguard, Borisov, who had been detained by the NKVD. After the shooting, Borisov was being driven to the Smolny Institute when he died in a motor accident; the others involved in the accident later disappeared.

Stalin reacted with alacrity. He immediately issued an emergency decree, without waiting for the approval of the Politburo, by which investigating agencies were to speed up their activities against those accused of crimes of terrorism. Judicial authorities were to show no leniency in such cases and the NKVD were to immediately carry out the death sentences thus bestowed. Stalin and his confidants then left for Leningrad, where he assumed personal control of the investigation.

Nikolayev meanwhile, when questioned as to his motives, hinted that the NKVD were involved, and that he had been a 'patsy'. He changed his story yet again, after Stalin arrived in Leningrad. Stalin was intent on proving that the assassination was part of a far-reaching conspiracy. He drew up a list of members of a 'Leningrad Terrorist Centre' and a 'Moscow Centre'. In return for the promise that his life would be spared, Nikolayev 'confessed' that he had killed Kirov on the orders of the Moscow Centre, as part of a plan that would lead to the murder of Stalin and other Party leaders.

The first mass executions in reprisal for Kirov's murder had already taken place. More than one hundred White Guards, arrested on trumped-up charges of terrorism, had been summarily tried and shot immediately after Stalin's decree. The members of the Leningrad Centre were tried at the end of December, before three judges, including the notorious Ulrikh; the prosecutor was Vyshinsky. The duo were to repeat the same routine on hundreds of occasions over the next decade. All the Leningrad group were found guilty and condemned to death. Nikolayev, too,

Stalin with Lenin

found that the promise that he would live counted for nothing: he was shot in the cellars at the Liteini prison.

The suspicion that the NKVD, and perhaps others, were involved in Kirov's assassination was given weight by subsequent events. Certainly the members of the NKVD who had been less than scrupulous in protecting Kirov were tried and found guilty of criminal negligence. But instead of execution, nearly all received light sentences. Yagoda, Commissar-General of the NKVD, treated them with unprecedented leniency, and when they were sent to the isolated gulag camp of Kolyma they were given easy jobs and many privileges. Three years later, at the height of the Terror, the men were taken back to Leningrad and shot. At his own trial in 1938, Yagoda admitted that he had ordered his Leningrad NKVD men not to obstruct Kirov's assassination. Yagoda said that he had taken his orders from a man called Yenukidze. Once a high-ranking Communist, Yenukidze was also for thirty-five years a close friend of Stalin's, was the godfather of Nadezhda Alliluyeva and later made the funeral arrangments after her suicide. But he had published a series of memoirs of the early revolutionary days, in which he failed to exaggerate Stalin's role. This was brought to Stalin's attention by various sycophants, and Yenukidze was hounded from office. By the time of Yagoda's trial, Yenukidze had already been shot as a spy and a traitor; it was merely a further act of spite that Yagoda should accuse him of the assassination of Kirov. Yenukidze had never possessed Yagoda's political clout. Inevitably, there was much to suggest that the

Trotsky

orders to permit – or even to arrange – the death of Kirov came from his old friend, Stalin.

Yagoda was himself shot, as was his successor in the post of Commissar-General. Though the NKVD was among the last of the Soviet elites that Stalin liquidated, every one of its senior officers eventually perished.

By 1936, there were 5 million in prisons and camps. By the end of 1938, this had swelled to 8 million. Another million had been executed outright, with at least 2 million dying in imprisonment. Stalin only signed the death-warrants of important figures. Stalin's evil dwarf, Yezhov, sent his master lists of names for his signature. Between 1937 and 1938, he sent 383 of these lists, containing 40,000 names. On a single day, 12

December 1938, Stalin signed away the lives of 3,167 prisoners.

Of the 139 Central Committee members, 110 were shot. Of a total of 499 senior military commanders, 436 were purged, most being executed and the remainder sent to camps.

Stalin began to compare himself not only to the ruthless modernizer of Russia, Peter the Great, but also to Ivan the Terrible, who had attempted to destroy the existing social order and create one based entirely on loyalty to himself. The effect of the Terror, which undermined all that had been achieved in the previous twenty years, was to silence all opposition to him.

NAZI-SOVIET PACT

Stalin's early behaviour towards Germany was highly contradictory. On the one hand, he knew that an ideological conflict was inevitable, and persistently refused to let himself be drawn into a military alliance; on the other, he continued supplying the Germans up to the night on which they attacked the Soviet Union.

Throughout the late 1930s, Hitler was un-equivocal about his future intentions. He intended to colonize the Soviet Union, but was concerned that Germany should not enter a war in the east until it was prepared militarily; to achieve this, Germany required raw materials from the Soviet Union. It was to this end that he engaged in prolonged diplomacy with Stalin.

Hitler also hoped that by signing the non-aggression pact with Stalin he might dissuade Britain from participating in a European conflict. He could renege on the agreement later. Stalin was drawn to the agreement through the opportunity it offered to acquire territory without great military commitment. Since the Red Army was depleted by the bloody purges of the 1930s (it was ill equipped, demoralized and badly led, 50,000 of the officer corps having been shot), Stalin determined to acquire a belt of defensive territory running from Finland to the Black Sea (he was to make eastern Poland the centre-piece) and to buy time.

The poor state of the Red Army was emphasized by the invasion of Finland, begun on 30 November 1938. Stalin had compelled the Baltic States to accept garrisons of Russian troops, but Finland refused his demand to move their border away from Leningrad and lease him the port of Hanko. In the ensuing winter war, the Soviet troops were outfought by the Finns under the formidable Marshal Mannerheim, and Soviet losses were immense. Only in February 1939, after prolonged bombardment and an attack by 140,000 troops, did Stalin prevail. This poor showing by the Red Army convinced Hitler that an early attack on Russia could not fail.

Poland was Hitler's major strategic consid-
eration. Control of the country offered both
a traditional channel for an attack on the east
and, if he waged war in the west, a defensive
buffer against an attack from the rear. Hitler
planned to attack Poland on 26 August 1939.
Throughout the summer he battled to isolate
Poland diplomatically, and calculated that
news of a Nazi-Soviet pact would deter
Allied intervention.

It was crucial that this pact should be
signed before the invasion. Stalin was
cautious; he was interested only in what
Russia might gain territorially, and to this
end a secret protocol was part of the
arrangement. In this, Germany agreed
that, in the event of the 'political transfor-
mation of eastern Europe', Poland would
be divided into German and Soviet spheres

of interest, and Stalin would have control
of the Baltic States. In late August, under
pressure to force the signing, Hitler was
compelled to write to Stalin personally.
When he received Stalin's favourable re-
ply, he exclaimed, 'I have them! I have
them!' The attack had to be delayed for
five days, but on 31 August the Germans
launched a blitzkrieg which swept away the
million – strong but antiquated Polish
Army within hours. Stalin thought he
had gained, when in fact the consequence
of co-operating in the destruction of Poland was to remove a major obstacle to the
invasion of the Soviet Union.

Within twenty-one months of the Nazi-
Soviet partition of Poland, approximately 2
million civilians had died. The SS murdered
the population in the western sector; in the

east, the Red Army pillaged the country and mounted a round of pogroms.

With Europe in turmoil, Stalin completed his annexation of the Baltic Republics in the summer of 1940. On 2 August 1940 they were incorporated into the Soviet Union. He was content to achieve his territorial goals off the back of the German successes in the west, and would not be drawn into a closer alliance with Hitler, who was anxious to turn Stalin's gaze from German military preparations in the west. In November 1940, Ribbentrop, Hitler's Foreign Minister, sought to seduce the Soviet Union into the Tripartite Agreement with Japan and Italy, persuade them to look away from Europe, and co-operate on a carve-up of the British Empire in the east. The meeting with Stalin's envoy,

Molotov, was conducted in an air-raid shelter. Ribbentrop insisted Britain was finished. The dour Russian listened carefully, and then said: 'If that is so, why are we in this shelter, and whose are these bombs that are falling?'

When Hitler realized that Stalin could not be distracted from Europe, he lost interest in negotiations and determined on a pre-emptive attack, though he was counselled continually that this would best be left until 1944. On 18 December 1940, he issued Directive No. 21 Operation Barbarossa, the invasion of the Soviet Union.

Hitler was distracted from this plan by Mussolini's failure in Greece, and by Yugoslavia, where army officers had rebelled against the regime's affiliation to the Nazis.

The brutal purges begin

The living quarters of a collective farm

But by the spring of 1941, the Germans had taken the Balkans and Greece, and were triumphant in Africa. Stalin was surprised at the speed of Germany's progress, but did not believe that Hitler was yet in a position to turn on him. He maintained deliveries of raw materials to Germany, and reaffirmed Russia's friendly intentions.

Throughout the spring of 1941 the inscrutable Soviet leader was repeatedly warned by American, British and by his own intelligence forces of an impending German attack. By late May, Marshal Zhukov could even identify the German units to be used, and their objectives. But Stalin ignored their warnings, and did not even show his generals the data he had received about German plans. He had made no plans for war and was intent on appeasement. He dismissed anything that did not fit in with his view of the situation as German propaganda, or British propaganda intended to force the Soviet Union into a war. He ordered his air force to allow the *Luftwaffe* to fly reconnaissance missions into Soviet territory without hindrance; it was as a consequence of this that most of the Soviet air force was later destroyed on the ground. Mobilization of the Red Army was ruled out.

In June, the British, who had cracked the German code, notified Stalin of the precise details of the German build-up. But he responded by issuing a public statement which decried the attempts of Britain to destabilize Soviet-German relations. On 21 June, the evening before the attack, Stalin denied Zhukov permission to mobilize, on the grounds that this would provoke. No

Soviet units had instructions as to orders in the event of hostilities. By the time Stalin unwillingly agreed to the issuing of war directives, the Germans had cut most communications, and the front-line Soviet units had no idea what was happening.

THE GREAT
PATRIOTIC WAR

In the early hours of 22 June, bombing attacks were launched on Sevastopol, Minsk, Kiev and the Baltic States. Stalin's generals tried to contact him, but were told he was asleep, and could not be disturbed. At 3.30 in the morning, Zhukov, who had Stalin's private telephone number, managed to get through to him; his news was greeted with disbelief. The Politburo finally met at 4.30. Stalin was pale and sick.

Starving peasants leave their land

Joseph Stalin

Operation Barbarossa was in full swing. Three German Armies, comprising 3.2 million men, and thirteen motorized divisions, including 3,350 tanks, supported by troops from Finland, Romania, Slovakia and Hungary, were carving up the Soviet Union. Army Group North made for the Baltic States and Leningrad; Army Group Centre headed direct for Moscow; and Army Group South was to take the Ukraine, overrun the industrial areas of the Dnieper, and take the Crimea and the precious oil reserves of the Caucasus.

Behind the orthodox troops went the *Einsatzgruppen*, the extermination squads sent to liquidate the 'Jewish–Bolshevik ruling class'. More than 300,000 civilians were killed in the first sixth months. Of the 5.7 million Russian prisoners taken, barely one million survived the war. The Germans had a genuine opportunity to exploit opposition to Stalin's regime and turn the Ukraine into an ally. But the policy of racist genocide prevailed, and all those they overran were motivated to fight tooth and nail.

The Germans could not afford a prolonged campaign in the east. Hitler had argued that the Soviet leadership would quickly collapse; the British had estimated that Soviet resistance to the Germans might be expected to last five or six weeks; in war-games, the Soviet generals, taking the German part had thrashed themselves. At first the Germans made great progress. The Soviet forces were poorly led and badly equipped, and Stalin himself suffered something of a nervous breakdown, retreating to his dacha.

But, within weeks, German progress slowed as resistance units, though cut off and disorganized, continued to fight furiously. Stalin recovered his nerve, reorganized his high command, rehabilitated crucial officers he had imprisoned and, though his arrogance caused him to make dreadful tactical mistakes, he increasingly took good advice, particularly from the great Zhukov, who saved him from disaster on many occasions. The Soviet Union also managed to relocate vital industries in Siberia, and went on to produce equipment to match that of the Germans – the T34 tank and the Yak fighter aircraft.

Hitler's generals were in favour of a mighty thrust at the centre of the Russian front to destroy the bulk of the Soviet armour, but Hitler maintained war on three fronts. As a consequence, Army Group North became deadlocked at Leningrad – a siege that was to last 900 days. In the south, the Germans progressed better; but Operation Typhoon, the main thrust at Moscow, to which 800,000 men were committed, did not take place until late in the year, by which time fatigue and the weather had taken their toll of both troops and equipment. The battle for Moscow opened on 15 November, and by 5 December, as temperatures plummeted to – 40°, the Germans had struggled to the outskirts of the city.

Stalin had by now come out into the daylight. Rejecting the language of socialism, he had called upon his fellow Russians to fight a Great Patriotic War. He refused to flee Moscow. Standing before the Kremlin, he reminded the Russians how they had so often before repelled the Teutonic Knights, the Tartars and the French. The effect was electrifying. The dusty bureaucratic spider, feared by all, was embraced as the national hero.

Outside Moscow the Germans came to a standstill. The Soviet command then released its strategic reserve of 700,000 troops in a decisive counter-attack which brought about a loss of confidence among the German generals. Hitler refused to allow them to retreat; they dug in and stabilized the eastern front. But German forces were now spread out in a line from the Baltic to the Black Sea. They had lost their momentum, and the wisest realized that they could not prevail in a war of attrition. They had already suffered 750,000 casualties.

In May 1942, misconceived Soviet plans to liberate the Crimea and raise the siege of Leningrad, both instigated by Stalin, resulted in catastrophic defeats. In June, Sevastopol fell and its army was destroyed by the Germans. Stalled in the north and centre, the Germans' summer attack – Operation Blue – had been to direct the bulk of Army Group South at the vital communications centre of Stalingrad. But with such good news elsewhere, Hitler was convinced that the Soviets were all but finished, and directed his forces to divide to both take Rostov and move on the Caucasus oil-wells. The attack on Stalingrad was ultimately left to Paulus's Sixth Army, supplemented by assorted Romanians, Italians and Hungarians of dubious worth. Aided by the *Luftwaffe*, the Germans reached the northern suburbs of Stalingrad on 23 August. Stalin refused to allow any retreat from Stalingrad,

The second Five-Year Plan is announced

Stalin made a pact with Hitler in 1939

and, led by Marshal Chuikov, the Red Army and improvised militia offered stern resistance. By the time German reinforcements arrived, their forces were embroiled in the most savage battle of the war. Amid street-fighting, and hand-to-hand combat fought in doorways, stairwells and basements, the city was reduced to a desolate ruin. But the Red Army successfully disrupted organized German manoeuvres, and on 13 September an all-out German attack to divide Soviet forces and drive through to the Volga failed. In late November Soviet forces completed a massive encirclement of the Germans and on 31 January Paulus and his staff surrendered, defying Hitler's orders to fight to the death; Hitler insisted that Paulus should have shot himself. The Red Army took more than 90,000 prisoners. The battle was the first major loss suffered by the Germans in Europe; the Red Army gained in confidence, and the Germans sensed defeat.

In the spring of 1943 the Germans straightened out their front line and made some gains, recapturing Kharkov. A major operation, Citadel, was planned for early summer. This would aim to encircle the concentration of Russian forces in the Kursk salient, between Moscow and the Sea of Azov, and drive through to Moscow again. But suspicions that the Allies were to attempt a landing in Italy caused the plan to be delayed until July. It the event, the Allies did invade Sicily. The delay allowed the Soviet Union to build up a massive concentration of forces in the salient; in April, there had been 1,200 Red Army tanks there, but by July this had swelled to more than 3,000.

Citadel was launched on 5 July. At the front of the German pincer movement were twenty Panzer divisions, including Hitler's pet Waffen SS units: SS Death's Head, SS Adolf Hitler and SS Das Reich. Little mercy was shown by either side. The Red Army was well dug in, and played to a plan, attriting the German forces until launching a counter-attack on 18 July. An extraordinary tank-battle erupted around Prokharovka, involving 1,000 vehicles. There were heavy losses on both sides, but at the conclusion the Germans had exhausted their reserves of men and armour, and were on the verge of a long retreat to Berlin. By the following January, Leningrad had been relieved. In April, German forces in the Caucasus were routed.

EXPANSIONISM

On 4 June the Allies occupied Rome. Two days later they landed in France. Rommel, who was in charge of coastal defences, was on his way to see Hitler when the news broke. Hitler was asleep, and no one dared disturb him. By the time he woke up in the afternoon and ordered that 'the enemy must be annihilated at the bridgehead by the evening of 6 June', the Allies were well ensconced. Within ten days, 600,000 troops were ashore; by the end of a month, nearly a million. Hitler could not accept it. He was convinced that the Allies could not hold together, that their alliance would collapse, that the British would fight the Russians, that his miracle weapons would destroy their spirit. In the east, the Russians advanced 300 miles in six weeks and expelled the Germans from their territory. They were only 400 miles from Berlin.

Stalin was determined to use the opportunity offered by the German defeat to extend the boundaries of the Soviet Empire as far west as possible. Thus, one by one, the historic capitals of Europe fell to the Red Army; and the longer the war went on, the better was Stalin's interest served. He nonetheless remained cautious in signalling his intentions to the West. As the Germans were driven from successive European states, the Soviets set up 'democratizing anti-Fascist fronts', political façades dominated by Communists, from which the future governments of those states might be derived.

Stalin's treatment of Poland was exceptionally brutal, though the Poles had never collaborated with the Germans. Stalin was determined that the nation which had often provided a corridor for the invasion of Russia (latterly through his own stupidity) should fall to Communism.

The Germans had disinterred the bodies of 15,000 Polish officers at Katyn. They claimed that the officers had been shot by Stalin after his annexation of eastern Poland. Stalin denied this (though it was certainly true) and retorted that the murders were the work of the Nazis and Polish collaborators.

Soviet soldiers resist a German offensive

Stalin meets with Roosevelt and Churchill

He used Katyn as a pretext to break off relations with the nationalist Polish Government in exile, and in July 1944, in preparation for the capture of Poland, set up the Polish Committee for National Liberation.

As the Red Army approached Warsaw, the government in exile faced the prospect of losing their nation to the Soviet Union. In Warsaw the Polish underground had long been preparing for an uprising to coincide with the liberation of the city. Now they were obliged to force the issue, to come out of hiding and hope to secure the capital before the Red Army arrived. The Warsaw uprising began on 1 August. Showing extraordinary courage, the Poles held the Nazis at bay for nine weeks, eventually retreating to the sewers. They were hunted down and gassed or drenched with petrol and set on fire. The SS slaughtered some 250,000 civilians, marched the surviving resistance members off to death camps, and demolished the ruins of Warsaw. Not a soul was left alive within the city. Throughout this, the Red Army was within striking distance; Stalin would not lift a finger to help those he termed Polish fascists, and forbade the Allies to intervene.

Stalin's desire to secure control of eastern capitals for political purposes, rather than bid for swift military victory, led to the Red Army becoming embroiled in a prolonged battle for Budapest in October 1944. The city was not taken until the following March, and it looked for a time as if the Red Army would fail to bring off the coup of taking Berlin before the Allies.

Soviet troops occupy Berlin in 1945

Millions grieved when Stalin died

balance of power in Europe, to have political and military forces capable of opposing the new Soviet imperialism. In October 1944, Stalin and Churchill had met in Moscow to discuss the post-war settlement. In the absence of the Americans, they had avoided the issue of borders, and had agreed more generally to create 'spheres of influence' – an acceptance that Europe, for the foreseeable future, would be devoid of its traditional powers. Churchill had given Stalin a piece of paper on which he had scribbled the suggestion that the Soviet Union be allowed to dominate in Romania and Bulgaria in return for accepting British interests in Greece and an equal share in the Balkans. Stalin ticked it; he never took much notice of paper agreements.

On 4 February 1945, Churchill, Stalin and Roosevelt met at Yalta in the Crimea to discuss how Europe might be stabilized after the defeat of Hitler. Though ostensibly a triumph of diplomacy, out of which came a call for the unconditional surrender of Germany, the Yalta conference was Stalin's high point.

Stalin was concerned only with the interests of his empire. He wanted to lay claim to all the territory that had traditionally been under Russian rule, and establish new European borders favourable to Russia. He wanted vast war reparations that would create a power vacuum in Germany; and he wanted Poland, the invasion corridor to Russia, to be left in a position from which it might be turned into a Soviet satellite.

Though Roosevelt was sympathetic towards Stalin, Churchill treated him with great suspicion. No new borders were decided upon. There was much talk of 'spheres of influence', and such ambiguity favoured Stalin's plans.

Even the demand for unconditional surrender worked in Stalin's favour: he was assured that the Germans could not surrender to the Western Allies in preference to the Soviet Union. Stalin had asked for the dismemberment of Germany. Though this was not agreed to, he kept up the pressure to utterly destroy Germany as a power by constantly accusing the Allies of fomenting peace-plans with the shattered Nazis.

In March 1945 Stalin received more good news. The Allied Supreme Commander, General Eisenhower, prided himself on not letting political considerations affect his operational planning, and, against the wishes of such as Montgomery, he told Stalin that the Allies' spring thrust in the west would be for Leipzig and Dresden, not Berlin. Stalin was delighted, and replied on 1 April, praising Eisenhower's strategy and saying that Berlin was, in any case, of no strategic importance. He then ordered his generals to beat the Allies to Berlin, using whatever means necessary.

The Red Army launched its final attack on Berlin on 16 April. A week later they were inside the city boundaries and shelling the Chancellery. Hitler committed suicide on 30 April. On 7 May, with the Red Army in charge of Berlin, and most of eastern Europe in Stalin's shadow, Germany surrendered unconditionally. The war had cost at least 50 million lives, 21 million of whom were Soviet citizens.

AFTER THE WAR

With the defeat of Hitler, the alliance between the West and the Soviet Union had served its purpose. Ideological differences and deep personal suspicions now surfaced in the matter of deciding what should be done to restore the ruined continent of Europe. The Americans, early on, raised the possibility of simply conceding control of eastern and south eastern Europe to the Soviet Union, accepting the partition of Germany, and forming a Western federa-

tion to run and restore the remainder. This, in effect, is what ultimately happened. But Stalin never sought to negotiate such a position openly. He achieved it piecemeal, and thus avoided any confrontation with the West. His methods were evident in the annexation of the German city of Breslau and the Silesian industrial area to Poland. The occupying Soviet forces simply placed these areas under Polish administration, and they consequently became part of the Soviet satellite system. This was presented to the Allies as a *fait accompli*; they could protest, but to do more would be dangerous.

Pre-war, and in the early days of retreat and defeat, Stalin had been a shadowy figure, loath to put himself out on a limb; he had refused to put his name to a single communiqué until the Red Army started winning.

But in the post-war euphoria, he allowed – indeed encouraged – his personal elevation to the status of Tsar. The Stalinist personality cult was born.

In victory, Stalin reverted to the terminology of old. He no longer called his citizens 'brothers and sisters', but 'Comrades'. He did not pay tribute to the Russian spirit for winning the 'Great Patriotic War', but ascribed victory to 'our political system'. It was business as usual, and the familiar paranoia returned. There were enemies, he said, both outside and within, who must be identified and, where possible, eliminated. The Soviet Union was economically devastated by the war and famine was widespread. Though Stalin saw no threat from a technically bankrupt Britain, the new Russian Empire was in no state to face up to the

economic might of America. Stalin determined that the world should not know the truth; the bogus statistics flowed again, and Churchill's 'Iron Curtain' descended across Europe.

More than 60 million Soviet citizens had endured Nazi rule. Those who had survived forced-labour, famine, extermination squads and partisan war now came under suspicion of collaboration. The NKVD began investigating, arresting and deporting *en masse*, sometimes uprooting whole peoples and transporting them to slow death in Siberia. Stalin set about tracking down every one of the 5 million citizens who had been displaced from the Soviet Union. He demanded from the Allies the swift return of all 2,500,000 members of the Red Army who had been taken prisoner by the Ger-

mans and were still alive. Since the Allies were keen to regain their citizens who had been captured by the Germans and were now in Soviet hands, they collaborated, however loathsome the business. The prisoners protested that they would be shot as traitors, and for many this proved the case. Others were sent to Siberia. Less than a fifth were allowed to return directly home.

Those military leaders who had carried Stalin's burden throughout the war were now considered a threat. Though Stalin did not shoot them out of hand, they were all quietly shifted to obscure appointments, even the incomparable Marshal Zhukov. The official histories now recorded that it was Stalin, and Stalin alone, who had won the war.

Several new creatures emerged. One was the unspeakable Beria. In 1946 the NKVD was split into the MVD (Ministry of the Interior) and the MGB (Political Police). Beria was not officially head of either, but in fact controlled both, together with the gulag slave-camp network and the counter-espionage organization, SMERSH. He was also a member of the Politburo. There was also Zhdanov, a career Communist, through whom Stalin initiated a purge of all Soviet artistic and cultural life.

Whatever the circumstances – personal or political, domestic or foreign – Stalin could only feel secure with a hegemony. His hopes for Soviet domination of Europe and the Near East were founded upon the collapse of the British Empire, which could no longer be economically sustained, and traditional

American policy in world affairs, which, provocation to war aside, was isolationist. Thus, in 1947, when the British announced that they would be withdrawing from India, Palestine, Turkey and Greece, Stalin had great hopes of expanding the Soviet sphere of influence. In this he was thwarted by the emergence of the Truman Doctrine, so-called after President Harry Truman, who, after pleas from the British, sent troops to Greece and Turkey, thus signalling that America recognized that it must assume the international – even imperial – mantle of Britain. It alone could oppose Soviet expansion; it too was threatened.

This move infuriated Stalin, and the Soviets co-operated even less over the question of rebuilding Europe. This needed American money, and Stalin was as keen for American aid as France and Britain. But he wanted it handed out unconditionally, so that his emergent satellite system would not be threatened by economic integration into any large-scale European plan; and he wanted Germany divided and left in penury. The co-operative plan for European regeneration evolved by American Secretary of State, George Marshall, was rejected by Stalin. The Soviet Union set about opposing the Marshall Plan through a programme of propaganda, psychological pressure and sustained subversion of the European nations, with the object of making political gains before the benefit of American aid might be felt, destroying the confidence of the West and forcing it to renegotiate; Communists fomented strikes, riots and political turmoil in France, Italy and, to a lesser extent, in Britain.

The eastern European countries were brought further into the fold. In Poland, the Polish People's Party was smashed, 100,000 of its members imprisoned and a number of its outspoken leaders murdered as a prelude to the creation of a single-party state. In Prague, in February 1948, the Communists staged a *de facto* coup, once again excluding all others from political power. Hungary, Romania and Bulgaria also turned from pink to red. Stalin failed to bring Tito to heel, and Yugoslavia was expelled from the new federation of Soviet satellites – the Cominform – for its nationalist deviancy. Stalin later ordered show trials and further bloody purges of the Communist hierarchy in the satellites to discourage any Titoism.

More than ever, the British and the Americans regarded the rapid rehabilitation of

Germany and its restoration as an economic power essential to stop Europe falling to Stalin. Stalin, in turn, knew that the Truman Doctrine and Marshall Plan were, as yet, tentative ventures by the Americans. If they could be forestalled, future American intervention might also be prevented. He hoped to apply pressure and sway American public opinion.

In March 1948, Stalin initiated a blockade of Berlin, which was divided into four sectors, three of them under Western control, the whole lying within the zone of Germany under Soviet occupation. It was both a test of Western nerve, to see if the new American doctrine would lead to active intervention, and an attempt to coerce the population of Berlin to vote themselves under Soviet rule.

But the city's nerve held, as did that of the Allies. Berlin was relieved by means of a remarkable airlift that fed the entire population from June 1948 to May 1949. Stalin was further thwarted by the formation of the North Atlantic Treaty Organization (NATO), and the Western resolve to go ahead with the restoration of Western Germany. By October 1950, Germany was two states.

Stalin looked to test Western resolve elsewhere. On 25 June 1950, Stalin gave the nod for North Korea, under Kim Il-Sung, to invade South Korea. Stalin was surprised at the vigour of the American response. Fortunately, he had taken the precaution of wiping his fingerprints from the affair. All Soviet advisers had been withdrawn from North Korea before the assault, and he refused to let Soviet troops participate. Rather, he managed to embroil China, and it was the Chinese who suffered losses of 750,000 men.

Stalin's final years were marked by the chill of the cold war abroad and deepening gloom at home, as he initiated yet another round of purges and encouraged the spread of anti-Semitism.

After his seventieth birthday he appeared listless, tired, unable to concentrate and obsessed with potential betrayal. His protective entourage was vast. When he travelled in his private train, there were guards posted every 100 yards along the side of the track. He showed little interest in the day to day running of affairs, made few speeches and, when he turned up for meetings, was overtly cynical about procedure. Most of the time he was at his dacha, sitting in the dark, smoking and watching films. Each night he surrounded himself with a party of high-ranking officials, with whom he would eat and drink until daylight.

His sedentary life, his smoking and the strains of work and conscience took their toll. In the early hours of 2 March 1953, after a veritable orgy lasting three days, Stalin suffered a stroke. He took three and a half days to die. Around his death-bed stood those sycophants and favourites who, by disguising their true feelings, had survived. Stalin died without a word of regret, having destroyed the hopes of socialism. Ironically, while his colleagues behaved like reprieved prisoners, the Soviet people mourned the man who had persecuted them for twenty years.

LIFE AND TIMES

Julius Caesar
Hitler
Monet
Van Gogh
Beethoven
Mozart
Mother Teresa
Florence Nightingale
Anne Frank
Napoleon

LIFE AND TIMES

JFK
Martin Luther King
Marco Polo
Christopher Columbus
Stalin
William Shakespeare
Oscar Wilde
Castro
Gandhi
Einstein